PRAYERS
for
PEOPLE
under
PRESSURE

Donald L. Deffner

NORTHWESTERN PUBLISHING HOUSE
Milwaukee, Wisconsin

Second Printing 1993

Library of Congress Card 92-60994
Northwestern Publishing House
1250 N. 113th St., Milwaukee, WI 53226-3284
© 1992 by Northwestern Publishing House.
Published 1992
Printed in the United States of America
ISBN 0-8100-0429-1

To
the members of
Immanuel Lutheran Church
Wichita, Kansas
whom my father
Dr. Louis H. Deffner
served from
1922-1965

A faithful people

Contents

Preface

Only you and God know fully the burdens you bear, the stresses and pressures you live under every day.

There are times when we are compelled to plead with God to change a difficult situation. "Intervene, O Lord!" Like Jacob wrestling with the angel, we cry, "I will not let you go unless you bless me" (Genesis 33:26). God encourages us to make specific requests (James 4:2).

And so we pray, "Answer me, O God, but in your own time, and in the name of him who said, 'Not my will, but thine be done.'"

But some trying circumstances will not change immediately, if ever at all. Then we are called to live under continuing stresses, and to learn that "just to endure is victory."

These prayers are written for such times.

Only the Spirit of God can teach us how to pray. These meditations are offered with the hope that you and I can better learn from the Master Teacher

> in the best of times
> and in the worst of times
>> to pray continually
>> to be thankful constantly
>> and to rejoice always.

Evening, and morning, and at noon, will I pray,
> and cry aloud: and he shall hear my voice (Psalm 55:17).

Acknowledgements

Credit is gratefully acknowledged for seed-thoughts from here and there from: Don Basham (1), Vicki Gardner, Don Wolkenhauer, Thomas P. Malone, Robert Roberts, Donna Preus, John Baillie (2), Duane Mehl (3), Margaret Wold (4), David Head, John Wesley, Martin H. Franzmann, Donald A. Tubesing (5), Reuben W. Hahn (6), Victor R. Gold, Brion Beetz (7), Paul J. Lindell (8), J. B. Phillips (9). Some of these are authors of books cited in the References (see back of book).

Some additional ideas stem from these sources which include both classics and contemporary works. (Numbers within parentheses indicate reference to a vignette in the manuscript.) Scripture references are generally listed in the order to which they are alluded in each vignette.

I also tender hearty thanks to Becky Kischnick and Jessica Wilmarth for a superb job at the computer.

Preparation for Stress

What a Day Ahead!

It looks like another day of stress Lord
Work piled up that never seems to end
Pressures from those who seek to control me
Unreasonable demands
even from those who love me
Responsibilities which sometimes seem beyond me
What do I do Lord?
Let me begin this day
by thanking you first of all
for *life itself*
My life
which *you* have given me
> *It is he who has made us*
> *and not we ourselves*

Then let me
by the power of your Holy Spirit
affirm my baptism
There you made me your child
and brought me into your family
and into eternal life
which I am in now
> *Fear not, for I have redeemed you;*
> *I have called you by name, you are mine. Behold,*
> *I have graven you on the palms of my hands.*

Now Lord
move those blessed assurances
from my head into my heart
and my hands
Empower me to act today
as your child
no matter what stressful situations
confront me
As others attempt to put pressure on me
move me to *react*
as your gentle loving servant

May I be a "little Christ"
when others confront me
throughout the day
O Lord
as I face what lies ahead of me
be my strength
my guard
my guide in everything I do
Keep me cool
when things heat up
Keep me tender
when I am inclined to be hard
Keep me resilient
when under pressure
Keep me faithful to you
in all things
In the strong Name of Jesus Christ

Psalm 5:3; 100:3   Isaiah 49:16   Proverbs 3:5

Beginning the Day

As I begin this day
let my first thought
be of your Name
I kneel before you
in worship adoration
and awe
I give you thanks
for all your wonderful gifts
to me and all generations
in the past
I confess my sin
not lightly
but with genuine sorrow
Forgive me Lord
through the merits
of the precious blood
of Jesus Christ my Savior
shed on the cross
My special requests
today are . . .
But according to thy will
O Lord
Thy will alone
preserve me now
from any forgetfulness
of you this day
In all the pressures
and stress ahead of me
let everything be passed
through the sieve of my faith
in your Son
When I am weak
let me fly to you
And when the day is ended
let me retire
to your arms
my eternal
Resting Place

Psalm 17:15; 130:5,6; 143:8; 92:1,2   Philippians 2:10

Getting Your Degree

O Lord rescue me
from the shameful sin
of sloth
and procrastination
Let this be
a glad bright day
of new beginnings
Let me meet every
challenge and opportunity
with renewed reliance
on your power
Rouse me to keep
the promises of yesterday
to right the wrongs
that remain unresolved
to finish the work
you have given me to do
that I may
run the course
redeem the time
finish the race
receive the crown
and by grace
accept the degree
W.D.
"Well done
good and faithful servant"

Ecclesiastes 9:10   2 Timothy 4:7-8   Matthew 25:21

O What a Beautiful Day!

Good morning Lord!
Now let not
the vigor of my spirit
or my apparent good health
and happy frame of mind
delude me into false reliance
on my self
Walk with me
every step of the way
Remind me that I am
wholly dependent on you
Let me remember
I am but a channel
of your grace
to others
When I think
may it be your thoughts
When I speak
may it be
your words I say
When I work
may it be
your work I do
Christ in me
and as I walk
through the day
may it be your path
I tread
serving others
not myself
as did
your Son[2]

Psalm 59:16,17; 90:14; 118:24; 119:147,148   Philippians 2:13

Always Ready

Lord let not
the tension of this time
the tightness of my schedule
the tautness of my mind
the urgency of the demands
upon me
(I have such plans made
Lord!)
blind me to the truth that
I may have no tomorrow
Let my plans be first
for today
readiness
watching
praying
knowing you could come
at
any
time

Matthew 24:42,44

Expect the Unexpected

When the unexpected happens
Lord
give me the grace to say
"Now what do you
have up your sleeve
today?"
Let me face the new
with excitement
rather than tension
with interest
rather than dread
with irony and humor
rather than fear
with stimulation
rather than
feeling threatened
With the Apostle Paul
let me affirm
"I can do all things
through Christ
who strengthens me"
In the Name of
the Father
and of the Son
and of the
Holy Spirit
   the Surpriser

Philippians 4:13

Who Follows in Their Train?

In sorrow suffering
pain or loss
O Lord
let me remember
the host of saints
who all have gone on
before me
and who passed through
the fire
The early martyrs

> *a noble army men and boys*
> *the matron and the maid*
> *Who follows in their train?*

Let me recall
all those faithful to you
through history
also my own relatives
loved ones and friends
who have gone on before

> *they rest from their labors*
> *and their works do follow them*

They met the test
They kept the faith
Let me now
I pray
emulate their example
in the crisis
which lies before me

> *O God to me*
> *may grace be given*
> *to follow in their train*

But most of all
O Lord let me
identify with your Son
who left me an example

that I should follow
in his steps
He endured the cross
despised the shame
O may I patient
bear his cross
and follow in
his train

Hebrews 12:1   Jude 3   1 Peter 2:21   Psalm 22:4,5; 44:1; 143:5   Revelation 14:13

That More Excellent Life

Lord thank you
for the gift of memory
with its moments
of delight
for the joys of yesteryear
which compensate
for the distresses
of today
But grant me
an avowed distaste
for living in the past
when opportunities for service
that more excellent life!
beckon me
in your world
today[6]

Luke 9:62   1 Corinthians 12:31   Philippians 1:10

Ready to Live—Ready to Die

The pastor turned around
at the altar and said
"And now let us pray
for the next one among us
who will die"
He was not melodramatic
but calm and earnest
and it struck me
Luther said
"If I were to die tomorrow
I'd plant an apple tree today"
Am I ready
to die
and to live
Lord?
Empower me
with your Holy Spirit
to be always prepared
for my own death
To live as though
I were going to die
tomorrow
or even today
but to work
for you
as if I had
a thousand years
to go!

Matthew 24:42   Philippians 1:23   Psalm 39:4-7; 31:14-16; 90:12

Coping with Stress —in times of testing

In the Middle of the Hurt

I am in the middle of the hurt right now Lord
Not physical pain this time but hurting
And there's not much I can do about it
    I feel so lonely Lord
    So powerless Lord
    So defeated Lord
I've done what you've told me to do
    in your holy Word
By the power of your Holy Spirit
    I've focused on you not on my own troubles
    I've prayed long and hard
    releasing my will to yours
    I've sought the counsel of Christian friends
    I've thanked you again today
    for your promises in my baptism
    that I am your redeemed and forgiven child
I know you love me Lord
    I know your Son traveled this path himself before
    and that he is with me now
But it still doesn't seem to be enough Lord
    So help me
    not to center on what I think I need
    but rather on what you know I need
    not to organize your answer for me
    but to await your direction
    not to be petulant but rather patient
    not to dwell on my pain but your promises
    but most of all to pray for your power to endure
Send your holy angels to me
    as you once sent them to your Son in his Gethsemane
Lift me up I pray by the power of him
    who was once lifted up
    on a cross
    for me
    And keep my eyes
    on that cross
    and not
    on my own

1 Peter 5:7   Hebrews 1:14   Revelation 2:10   Psalm 25:15-18

Depressed? Laugh and Sing!

Lord give me the courage
the heavenly medicine
to sing
when I am in the prison
of depression
as the apostles did
in jail
To laugh
at the demons within me
knowing you
reign supreme
in the throne room
of my heart
To be thankful
at all times
knowing you
are in control
Christ in me

Acts 16:23-25   Psalm 27:6; 40:1-3   Ephesians 5:19,20

When the Anger Begins

Dear Lord
I can feel
the frustration setting in
my blood pressure rising
the anger welling up
And hatred
is waiting at the door
to be let in
My flesh is weak
I am about to fall
But "willpower"
is not the answer
For like St. Paul
though I will
to do good
instead I do evil

Rescue me O God
from my foes
beginning with
myself
Fill me with
Your Self
Patience
Calm
Gentleness
Sweet Reasonableness
and the Peace
you alone can give
Now
I await
your Presence

Psalm 37:8   Romans 7:19-25   1 Corinthians 2:14-16

How Do I Decide, Lord?

I'm under pressure
to decide
Which way to go
Lord?
I want to follow
your will
in my choice
One friend
supported my indecision
by saying
"Don't just do something
Stand there!"
But another said
"Sometimes it's better
to be sorry
than safe"
Give me the counsel
of your Word
O Lord
and give me
wise Christian friends
and then
the courage
to act
to dare
to risk
to reach for
the trapeze
and leap
knowing that
your everlasting arms
are there

Joshua 24:15   Deuteronomy 33:27   Psalm 19:7-10

Learning How to Wait

This time
I want to act
to make a decision
But the Spirit
in your Word
tells me to wait
on you first
to hear *your* counsel
For if I don't wait
I won't have
my strength renewed
Purge me of impatience
O God
Instead of a rash temperament
give me wisdom
Show me *your* plan
and not my own
Move me to seek
that peace of mind
which comes not
of my own design
but yours
that your peace
which passes
all understanding
may fill my heart
and mind

Psalm 27:14; 69:13   Philippians 4:7

To Endure Is Victory

Lord I'm too hassled
to think clearly
Too bruised
to be "spiritual"
Too defeated
to pray
I don't feel much like
"a victorious Christian"
but in the emptiness of my soul
let me not grieve
or think that
my dilemma means defeat
Rather let me find you
Master Teacher
Then instruct me
to look not for
success but faithfulness
Not for immediately answered prayer
quick answers
happy solutions
instantaneous transformation
the holy spectacular
but rather the availability
of quiet daily grace
and the perfect peace
that tells me
just to endure
is victory¹

Psalm 32:6,7; 40:1-3   Revelation 2:10

Dependency—on What or on Whom?

When I feel
the necessity
to eat more
to take another drink
or another pill
divert my craving
O Lord
to a greater need
for *you*
Take my suffering
deterioration and helplessness
and make my
"bottoms up"
not
"one more for the road"
but rather a
hitting bottom
which results in my
total dependence
on you
that by the power
of your Spirit alone
I may experience
Christ's resurrection
in my life
and look not
elsewhere
but always see you
face to face

Psalm 73:26   1 Corinthians 13:12   Psalm 123:1,2; 141:8

What a Flood!

Lord move me
from the "why"
of suffering and crisis
to the "how"
of ministering
to others
By your Spirit
ignite the fuse
the chain reaction
of your power
within me
which begins with
rejoicing in suffering
which then produces
endurance
from which comes
character
followed by hope
and then the pouring out
of your Holy Spirit
within me
What a flood![4]

Colossians 1:24   Romans 5:3-5

Worry

Lord
teach me
not to worry
when I can
pray

Psalm 17:6-7; 42:5; 91:15   1 Peter 5:7

Give Me Some Answers!

I want some answers
Lord
clear directions
final solutions
but without
too much anxiety
or pain
on my part
But my demands
are wrong
Instead awaken me
to the biblical truth
that *discovery*
may only come
through *crisis*
distress
grief
even agony
and that
as I share in
your sufferings
and those of others
I also receive
your comfort

Philippians 3:10   Romans 5:3   1 Peter 4:13

Getting the Proper Focus

Lord direct me
not to focus my concern
on my stress
and anxiety
but rather
on *you*
Let me thankfully realize
that all in my daily walk
which is
good true lovely
heartwarming
joyous
exhilarating
comes
from *you*
Let my dreams
and aspirations
lead me upward
to *you*
that I may
be filled with
wonder admiration
awe
and worship
of *you*
Then the pressures
will be put
in proper perspective
the focus clear
the picture in
true proportion
you[9]

Philippians 4:8   Psalm 25:15; 27:7-9

Christ Our Passover Is Sacrificed for Us

When stress afflicts me
O Lord
let me recall
the unfathomable agony
of your Passion
your suffering and death
on the cross
for me
Let me realize
how infinitesimal
is my pain
compared to yours
for my sin
But allow me to share
in the gracious benefits
of your sacrifice
that I may not only receive
the forgiveness of my sin
but the secret
of your power and peace
Then may I participate in
the sufferings of others
and at last receive
the undeserved gift
of the life
to come

1 Peter 4:13; 5:1   Hebrews 13:3   Revelation 2:10b

From Christmas to Easter

During my struggle
O God
grant that I may
go to Bethlehem
and there enfold
my Savior
in the manger
of my faith
During my struggle
O God
grant that I may
go to dark Gethsemane
and Calvary's mournful
mountain climb
and share in
his sufferings
for my transgressions
God's own sacrifice complete
During my struggle
O God
grant that I may
go to the garden
see the empty tomb
and through faith
in my resurrected
and ascended Lord
rise above
my passing trial
and at last
win the victory
through Christ
my Lord

Colossians 3:1   Hebrews 13:14

At the Death of a Friend

O God I know
yours was the first tear to fall
when my friend died
Because of our sinful state
death reigns in this world
So comfort us Lord
with the certain hope
of life to come
Turn our mourning
into dancing
and weeping into joy
knowing the resurrection
is near
And teach us so
to number our days
that we are always ready
And not just now
as the family nods
in stunned grief
but in the weeks to come
move me Lord
in true compassion
to aid the bereaved
with a *ministry of presence*
and the assurance
of your sacred promise
that our loved one is forever
"with the Lord"!

Psalm 116:15   Romans 5:12   Psalm 30:5b,11,12; 126:6; 90:12; 39:4-7   1 Thessalonians 4:17

Meeting the Test

I was facing a test the other day Lord
A test of my ability
and a test of my faith in you
And I prayed for *control*
And you came through again
I met the test
by your grace
I thank and praise your Name
Now please give me the grace
not to rest on my laurels
but to rely on your power
and grace
If the time of trial is not today
I know it will come
For you have said
You test those whom you love
those who are your children
Otherwise we are not really
your children
For when we are tested
we are drawn nearer to you again
So keep me in your grace
again this day
But while I am on the mountain top
prepare me for the valley
While I am calm
prepare me for the time
of unrest and disturbance
While I am confident now
prepare me for the hour
of doubt and depression
While I am strong
prepare me for the day of weakness
O God
who sees my downfalling

and my uprising
who knows all that my life
has in store for me
guide me in my Christian walk
Let me not worry about tomorrow
but rather put my trust in you
Tomorrow will have enough
worries of its own
By your grace
be present with me now
and accept my thanks
for the joy and exhilaration
which fills my heart
Praised be the name of the Lord

1 Corinthians 10:13   Hebrews 12:6   Matthew 6:34

A Way Out

Every temptation
that has come my way
is the kind
that normally comes
to people
For God keeps his promise
and he will not allow me
to be tempted
beyond my power
to resist
but at the time
I am tempted
he will give me
the strength to endure it
and so provide me
with
a way out

1 Corinthians 10:12,13

Stress and the Cell of Suffering

Lord
sitting in my cell
of suffering
though I think
I am alone
let me try the door
and see
it has been unlocked
all the time
You have been waiting
outside to greet me
with your wisdom
about my pain
its purifying
and its blessing
Give me
your perspective
O Lord
What I thought
was punishment
is now mercy
What I thought
was a pit
is a well
of your merciful presence
What I thought meaningless
puzzling and mystifying
now has purpose
For I am
closer to you
O Lord
Now
through piercing tears
I see your pierced hands
and side

Though wounded
I see wounds
you bore
for me
Through pain
I better see
myself
sitting by your side
through all eternity[8]

Jeremiah 29:11   Isaiah 26:3   James 1:2   1 Peter 4:12,13   2 Corinthians 4:17,18
Ephesians 2:4-6

The Semaphore of Stress

Lord even as
funeral sermons
are not for the dead
but for the living
let the stress of grief
be for me
a signpost
of the transient nature
of life
a semaphore
to prepare me for
my own death
and that of
my loved ones
a harbinger
of the hope
to come

Matthew 24:3,42

On the High Wire

Make me
a high wire artist
O Lord
skillfully balanced
between time
and eternity
When I am in
good health
remind me
it is but temporary
Pain and sorrow
old age and death
will come
I'm just not handicapped
now
But divest me
of morbidity
Give me zest
and vividness
exulting in
the vigor of life
Make each day
a joyous adventure
knowing I tread this wire
but once
Give me therefore
I pray
both satisfaction
and detachment
the perfect
balancing act

Philippians 1:21-26   Psalm 33:20-22; 95:1,2   Philippians 4:4

On the Loss of Good Health

When stress sets in
because my health fails
O Lord remind me
of that which I
should never have forgotten
My birth was only a portal
to a life which is but mortal
My illness is a signal
along the way
Prepare me to surrender
to the earth
from which I came
not morbidly
but with reality
Meanwhile
grant such good health
to this earthly frame
as you will
Give me wise stewardship
in caring for
your living temple
And with this
calm of mind
may I await
the new body
you will give me
with no stress or distress
no tears or death
no sorrow or crying or pain
in
The New Jerusalem[8]

Psalm 90:12   1 Corinthians 6:19; 15:51-58   Revelation 21:4

The Fellowship of Suffering

O God prevent me
from the pretentiousness
of thinking I am unique
in my suffering
and from a self-pity
that I am alone
in my struggle
Move me
by your Spirit
to seek out
the fellowship of
burden-bearers
my comrades of the cross
Reveal to me
my affinity
with those distressed
throughout the world
that we
knit together in love
may share
in Christ's sufferings
and be like him
in his death
Make me not only
a burden-bearer
but a
burden-sharer

Philippians 1:3-5; 3:10   Colossians 2:2,3   Galatians 6:2

A Fountain Overflowing

Lord
keep me from being
a masochist
or a martyr
demonstrating my distress
parading my pain
proud of my patience
before others
Let me rather be
poured out
spilled over
a fountain overflowing
the Christ in me
that others may see
him
and not myself
All glory
be to you
O Lord[8]

1 John 2:6   2 Corinthians 4:8-11

Just Can't Keep a Secret

After the stress is gone
O Lord
let me recall
your goodness
in delivering me
But let me not
keep secret
your salvation
but tell the Good News
to all
that they also
may rejoice
and glorify your name
and come to you
in time of need

Psalm 18:6,19; 40:9,10,16; 50:15; 52:8; 66:16-20; 73:28   Acts 4:20

The Cure for Restlessness

When I'm restless
Lord I pray
that I bear
all things today
and your power
come be with me
now
and through
eternity

Psalm 16:9; 116:7   Isaiah 6:16   Matthew 11:28-30   2 Thessalonians 1:7   2 Corinthians 12:9

A Deed Indeed

Move me
in my stress
O Lord
to consider
the hurt
of others
But not only
to think
but to act
a phone call
a letter
a visit
a deed of love
bearing them
up
as you bore
all
for me[8]

Galatians 6:2   1 John 3:18

Hurt but Healed

O Lord
You allow hurt
but bring healing
You permit pain
but cause relief
You send stress
but also your Spirit
You test me
but strengthen me
You reprove me
but encourage me
You try me
but never deny me
Your power
is boundless
O Lord
Blessed be
the name of the Lord!

Lamentations 3:22,23   1 Corinthians 10:13   Psalm 72:18,19

The School of Suffering

Lord I pray
for healing
from my ills
if it be
your will
But spare me of
an idle hope
of life that's free
from misery
Let me rather
go to school
with you
be your true disciple
and learn from you
surrender to
accepting stress
and pain and death
and daily die
with you
Then I can pray
for that Great Day
for which my eyes
look to the skies
to be with you
forever[8]

Matthew 11:29   Romans 6:3-11   2 Corinthians 4:10-12

In the Hospital

Lord make this building
your house
of healing and of hope
my bed your footstool
my doctors and nurses
your ministering angels
my illness the robe
you have given me
to wear
but most of all
the dwelling place
of him who is
my daily fare
who's always there
your gift so rare
that Blessed One
himself who bare
and chose to dare
in loving care
his life to spare
for me[8]

Isaiah 66:1   1 Peter 2:24   Romans 8:32

Unconditional Surrender

Lord teach me again
the hard lesson
I so soon forget
that since your call
is really for all
and not just part
of me
to accept pain
rejoice in the midst of suffering
sing when in
the prison of despair
continually give thanks
and be content with
what I have
Lord
since now I see
your wish for me
is not a cup
still partly full
but rather that
it empty be
teach me again
that ne'er will I
replenished be
until I see
and bend my knee
before the One
Who died for me
the *Christ in me*

Ephesians 2:8,9   2 Corinthians 12:9   Colossians 1:27

Grasping the Moment

Lord
after I have cried
to you
from the depths
of despair
and after you
have answered
my prayer
let me not dismiss
that moment
when stress has passed
and pain at last
is gone

Let me snatch it
and not miss it
ere it slips
through my mind
that little liberation
that mini-resurrection
which is a sign
a presage a foretaste
of that Great
Resurrection ahead

Let my sigh of relief
be my sign to debrief
all my sorrow and grief
in the light of
that Great Day
to come[8]

Psalm 130:1; 22:24   Romans 8:11   Revelation 21:4

Coping with Stress
—in relation
to others

"For God's Sake, Love Me!"

O God
move me to realize
that my emotional problems
may arise not because
I am not loved
but because
I have not loved
others enough
Motivate me
to give up my complaints
and my unhealthy cries
To love more
To serve more
In short
to be like your Son
who came
not to be ministered unto
but
to minister

Matthew 20:28

An Aching Heart

Lord teach me
that I cannot ache
for someone else
unless I know
what suffering is
myself[a]

Galatians 6:2   Hebrews 13:3   2 Corinthians 1:7

Poisonous Weeds

Forbid me Lord
from praying for my enemies
or those who wronged me
while cherishing
the secret wish
that they be hurt
or destroyed
Purge me of
bitterness anger
revenge hate
Root out
the poisonous weeds
of jealousy
entangled in my heart
towards those
who have a greater position
than the small place
I occupy
I am self-centered
wooden powerless
Lord
to make this change
infuse me with
your Holy Spirit
that I may truly
love my enemies
bless
and not curse them
and pray for them
wholeheartedly
as did your Son
upon the cross

Psalm 37:7   Matthew 5:44   Romans 12:19-21

The Demons Within

Lord help me
to recognize
the demons
within me
anger
resentment
a complaining nature
criticism
self-pity
the desire to dominate
and control other people
the inclination
to manipulate
their behavior
for my own purposes
and designs
Let me rather
with courage and humility
turn others over
to you

Romans 7:17,18   Romans 8:6-13

Emotions That Disturb

Relieve me not
O Lord
of those emotions
which should continue
to disturb me

Ache
> for the pain of others

Pity
> for the poor
> that moves me to act

Shame
> when I think of
> how little I have done
> for you

Alarm
> when I would rather die
> than have the courage
> to live

Stress
> when I think of
> your Cross

And give me
Peace
> that I may order
> my soul aright and

Compassion
> that I may will
> to do
> the right

John 9:4

A Clean Slate

O Lord
let not the
weight of forces upon me
the frustrations
with which I struggle
or the critical decisions
I must make
be my *rationalization*
for sins against others
against you O Lord
Recall my trespasses
before my eyes
the evil thoughts
the loveless words
the unkind deeds
the duty left undone
that I may see
and repent
But then O Lord
by your grace
erase them from
your memory
and mine
and teach me also
to forgive
and forget

Psalm 51:10,11,17   Isaiah 43:25   Colossians 2:13,14

That Person!

How insensitive that person
is to others!
How blatantly
manipulative
always trying
to *control*
How cold and
heartless at times
lacking in compassion
domineering
lording it over others
strutting around
defensive
quick-tongued
complaining
hardly the soul
of gentleness
and peace
and love
Lord
help me realize
when
I
am
"that person"

1 Corinthians 10:12   Romans 12:3   Galatians 6:3

Peace Be Within This House!

Lord purge me of
the hypocrisy
of being patient with others
outside my home
but petulant
complaining and bitter
when I am with
my loved ones
When the pressures
of this day
are over "out there"
by your grace
let me not dump
all my frustrations
anger and despair
on those nearest
and dearest to me
Forgive me for
the besetting sin
of self-centeredness
within my own walls
Make me
courteous gentle tender
uncomplaining kind
outgoing and
generous in spirit
not a brooder
Pure in motives
not pouncing on others
or taking advantage
of those in my care
but denying myself
Not a strife maker
but a peacemaker
Not a bear

but one who bears
the burdens of others
especially
my own
beloved family

Philippians 2:2-5   Galatians 6:2

Celebrate Your Calling

Lord give me grace
to resist the pressures
of those who
urge me to marry
or not to marry
Give me the courage
to affirm and rejoice in
that calling in life
which is pleasing
to your holy will
If I am not a mother
or a father
let me be a parent
to those who are
parentless
Empower me
to be my own person
that is
the person
you
want me
to be

Romans 12:1,2

Handling a Quarrel

During a heated argument
O Lord
give me the power
which I don't have
to control my anger
and see my own
self-righteousness
and my canny knack
of seeing a chink
in the other person's reasoning
that I might move in
for the kill
Keep me cool Lord
but not cold
Patient
but not calculating
Willing to bear
hate-filled words
as you did
not arrogantly
but knowing my own
self-centeredness and pride
Put the words into my mouth
I cannot muster alone
Teach me to listen
and not to dominate
To win the peace
not the argument
Help me to know
that persons in
their overwhelming pain
and glowering mien
often say the things
they do not really mean
Empower me to take

the last cutting words
in silence
if I must
yes I must
And let there be
forgiveness
reconciliation
trust once more
the healing
you alone
can give

Psalm 12:3,4; 34:13,14; 73:1; 130:4; 141:3   James 3:5-18

Go Ahead—Get Angry

O Lord I know
I cannot keep Satan
from shooting arrows
of evil thoughts
into my heart
but by your grace
I can keep them
from sticking
and growing there
It is not a sin
to be tempted
but to yield
to that enticement
Grant me the grace then
to experience anger
but not to sin
by letting it grow
in my heart

Ephesians 4:26   1 Corinthians 10:13

Getting the Big Picture

Lord help me realize
there are some situations
I can't control
and some I can
Like an argument
When there's a misunderstanding
Lord
give me calm emotions and
a rational mind
attuned to your Spirit
Let me see
The Big Picture
enframing my adversary
in compassion and kindness
sensitivity and concern
Let me not harass
but heal
Not twist the knife of attack
but gently withdraw it
Make me a sponge
a set of ears
for the other
By your Spirit
energize us
to share our humanity
affirming mutual support
And though we disagree
give us the grace
of shared respect
as your beloved creations
Help us to
avoid the bonfire
of self-consuming retaliation
and may we rather
be warmed

by the shared blessing
of your radiant presence
our dialogue
a table spread
for an event
of care
and communion
with you[7]

Romans 12:10   1 Corinthians 13:4-7   Ephesians 4:32

Stop Forcing Me!

When others pressure me
to do that which
I don't want to do
give me the wisdom
O Lord
to distinguish
between my justifiable freedom
and a spirit of
sheer stubbornness
just wanting to have
my own way
In yielding to
what you
would have me do
let me be
malleable not malevolent
cooperative not cantankerous
receptive not resentful
Let me incarnate
grace under pressure
the good of others
rather than the gain
of my own pride
for the sake of him
who gave up everything
for me

Philippians 2:1-4   Ephesians 4:1-3   Colossians 3:12,13

On Serving Others

When serving others
wearies me O Lord
let me remember
him who poured himself out
for our sake

When my head aches
let me remember
him who had no place
to lay his head

When my back is breaking
let me remember
the stripes he bore
for me

When my arms
and legs hurt
let me remember
him whose hands and feet
were nailed to the cross
for me

When I am put down
mistreated
slandered
cursed
let me remember
him who was
despised and rejected of men

Let me share
in his sufferings
O Lord
a servant
even unto
the cross

Ephesians 6:5,6   Matthew 6:20   Isaiah 53:5   Romans 8:28-30   Philippians 2:4-8; 3:10

Stress from Fear of Others

O God
be not far
from me
when I fear
other people
Remind me
they are all
like I am
as grass
They wither
They die
They come naked
from the womb
and naked
they return
They all must bow
before you
So unless you are
on my side
I falter
But I will not fear
You are my stronghold
my refuge
You will deliver me
O Lord
Praised be
the name of the Lord!

Psalm 118:5-9; 71:12; 103:15-18   Job 1:21   Psalm 124; 9:9; 18:1,2

Revenge!

Lord when I desire
revenge
keep me from proudly withdrawing
thinking I am
obeying your law
by not avenging myself
while really I wait
and salivate
for your dire wrath
upon the one
who wronged me
But let me rather
prepare a glorious banquet
and fill the glass
of my tormentor
in love
not hypocrisy
that by your blessing
evil may be overcome
by good
For if I cannot
bear evil
then I am
soundly conquered
by it

Psalm 119:53; 15:1-3   Romans 12:19-21

Not Loquacious but Listening

Pinch me
Shake me
Awaken me
out of the delusion
that I am a
"solo Christian"
O Lord
Impel me to seek
the wise counsel
of others
especially those
seasoned veterans
of the cross
far more advanced
in spiritual understanding
than I
Teach me how to be
not loquacious
but a listener
To bare my defeats
before them
that I may learn
how you have worked
through them
and granted them
the victory
which is also
mine
through Christ
the Victor

Romans 12:15; 15:1,2   Galatians 6:2   Psalm 22:4,5

On Releasing My Children

First they were babies
so dependent
Then "the little ones"
Then "the boys" or
"the girls"
Now they're adults
I still feel constrained
to instruct
to guide
to mold
yes at times to
control them
Lord give me
the balance
to love
but not to smother
to dialogue
but not to dictate
to listen
but not
that I might better
manipulate
to *trust*
knowing how much
you love them too
to *release* them
to you

Psalm 13:1,5,6; 22:24-26; 38:9   1 Peter 5:7

The Mystery of Intercession

Am I praying enough
for other people
Lord?
I pray not to
control their lives
But in my concern
for what is best for them
in your Grand Design
intervene
O Lord
with the
divine adroitness
of your lucid love
In the mystery
of my intercession
and your divine expertise
do that
I pray
which is beyond
our comprehension
or ability
to understand or effect
Release your power
Unleash the unfathomable
miracle of your wisdom
that we may
exhilarate with you
in heavenly hilarity
at the masterstroke
of your marvels[9]

Romans 8:26-28   Psalm 5:11,12

Coping
with Stress
—in relation
to my work

Stress Management

Lord teach me
that stress comes not
from *outside* pressures
(that I might rationalize)
but from *within* me
I am responsible
By your power
let me learn
with St. Paul
how stress can do more
for me
than *to* me
By your Spirit
counsel me
so that crises
may not conquer me
Let stress be harnessed
to give me energy
and enthusiasm
to grow and learn
and work harder
for you
That apparent evil
may be turned
into good
And I may discover
that when I am weak
then you are strong
through
Christ in me[10]

1 Corinthians 12:9,10   Colossians 1:27

The Struggle to Get Ahead

Sometimes
the squeeze is on me for
higher profits
longer hours
increased productivity
closing the deal
even if you must
"cut some corners"
"lie a little"
"cut the other person out"
"—That's business"
What do I do Lord?
I'm caught in the middle
I need my job
and family security
How does a Christian survive?
Lord keep me ever mindful
that my true Master is you
and there is *no* security outside of you
No matter what the cost
make my business ethics
always those of your kingdom
righteousness godliness
faith love
endurance gentleness
And if I lose
let it be
a "loss" to the world
but a gain for Christ
And if material blessings
come my way
Let me know that
it is your gift
a trust of which
I am steward

But let my true riches
lie in good works
empowered by your Spirit
a generous and sharing nature
and the goal
of living in
your eternal Kingdom

Luke 3:14   James 4:13-16   1 Timothy 6:6-21   Philippians 3:7-11; 4:11   Matthew 6:19,20

Getting a Good Hold

When I am pressed
to grab and
to get
rather than to give
to tighten my hold
on what I have
move me to
release my grasp
on what is transient
and reach out
for that which is
lasting
For here there is
no continuing city
A stranger and pilgrim
am I
Direct my eyes
homeward
to you
Give me
the
eternal perspective

1 Timothy 6:19   Hebrews 6:18   1 Timothy 2:11   Hebrews 12:2

Pressure to Succeed—Freedom to Fail

Lord make me
at peace with "failure"
when it comes my way
Don't let the world around me
squeeze me into its mold
of values
Rather let me join
the apostle-band of "failures"
who surrounded you
Let me follow
the greatest "Failure" of all
to the cross
so that assimilated
identified
penetrated
by his victory
I may see
gain come out of loss
good come out of
apparent evil
hope come out of
seeming defeat
And Lord
give me the goal
not "to succeed"
but to be *faithful*
at all times
to you

Psalm 106:34,35   Philippians 3:7-11

Pious Prayerbook Reading

This day
as the pressures to conform
to this world's values
assail me
let me ask
"What would Christ
have done?"
Then let me be
patient not intolerant
compassionate not cold
eager to serve
not indolent
gentle towards others
not hard or rash
calm in spirit
not restless
faithful to you
in all things
Keep me
from just nodding
in devout agreement
as I piously read
this prayerbook
but to *do*
to *act*
to *live*
as did your Son
Christ in me

Romans 12:1,2   1 John 3:18

Distress vs. Discernment

Put my priorities
in order Lord
Teach me from your Word
that who I am
is worth much more
than what I do
The uncontrollable
is in your hands
My body
is your temple
Hope in you
can outlast
the direst
of circumstances
You never give a problem
without a promise
So let me live
with present challenges
rather than
grieving over the loss
of past treasures
Not contentious
for the things
of this world
but always content
in you[5,10]

Matthew 6:33   1 Corinthians 6:19,20   1 Corinthians 10:13   Luke 9:62   1 Timothy 6:6-8

Grief, the Teacher

Lord instruct me how
to make peace with pain
to make grief my teacher
not my conqueror
Lord help me
to acknowledge grief
its necessity
its natural process
for my healing
to see that grief
is not the problem
but the solution
to my hurt
Let me reinvest myself
in the new incentives
you place before me
Let the mended link
in the chain of my strength
be stronger than before
a new bond of courage
empowering me
and helping others to be
ever more closely
fused with thee

2 Corinthians 12:10   Philippians 1:12-14

The Winner!—First Prize!

When recognition
comes my way
O Lord
let me not yield
to the puffed up feeling of pride
thinking there is some
quality within me
an innate superiority
over others
For then comes
my fall
Give me rather
true humility
sober judgment and
heartfelt thanks to you
for such gifts
as I have
And always the grace
to proclaim
"Not to me
not to me
but to your name
be the glory!"

Proverbs 16:18; 29:23   Romans 12:3   James 4:6   Psalm 115:1

Work Your Work that I May Work

I know *you*
> draw me into the
> crucible of conflict

I know *you*
> test and try me
> in the valley
> of pain and sorrow

I know *you*
> allow me to taste
> the agony of affliction

I know *you*
> give my enemies permission
> to oppose and oppress me

I know *you*
use these things
> to purge and prepare me
> for *your* purposes

So then work *your* work
> in me O God
> that I may be
> better prepared
> by *your* Spirit
> to work
> for *you*

John 6:28,29   Ephesians 3:20,21   Psalm 90:17

The Right Kind of Pressure

When things
are going well
and the heat
seems to be off
(at least for now)
challenge my complacency
Lord
Press me with
the questions
and answers
I must never forget
Who will listen
to the pain and hurt
of others?
I will

Who will visit
the distressed and lonely?
I will

Who will feed
and clothe the needy?
I will

Who will bring
the Word of Life
to those without it?
I will

When a knock comes
on my door
move me not only
to say
"Arise, the Master comes!"
but also to
go out that door
pressed into your service
to many who
are under greater stress
than am I

Matthew 25:45

A New Pair of Glasses

Give me the insight
O Lord
to see
when my work
or other individuals
are not the problem
but *I* am
Prevent me from
running scared
distrusting people
heading for hopelessness
so blinded by burdens
of my own
that I blame others
rather than myself
Give me the eyes
to recognize
the trusted friends
I have
but most of all
You
the Friend of sinners
Forgive my myopia
and restore the utopia
of a clearer vision
of my work
my comrades
and you
Give me
the spectacles
of your Spirit[7]

1 Corinthians 2:14-16   Matthew 11:19   Luke 2:29,30

Just Plain Exhausted

I'm tired Lord
drained

just plain exhausted

But now let me not
just dwell on my weariness
but on your strength
Direct me to
your holy Word
O you who were
wearied for our sakes
even to the cross
Let me find my refuge
in you
Send your holy angels
to minister to me
and bear me up
Refresh renew and strengthen me
Give me the peace
the world cannot give
Restore to me
the joy of your salvation
you have promised
you will come
Abide with me then
till I find my final rest
in you

*Isaiah 40:30,31   Hebrews 1:14   Psalm 91:12   John 14:27   Psalm 51:12; 116:7
Matthew 11:28*

The Rat Race

When I am weighed down
with the stress of
ceaseless toil
endless miles
interminable typing
numberless meals
multiplying meetings
changeless chores
help me
fix my eyes on you
O Lord
Let me see
that the meanest task
is sacred when done
in your name
Nothing is purposeless
in your sight
And when boredom monotony
tedium and dreariness
set in
Assure me that you
are at my side
Let me thank you
for the ability to work
and know my work is done
directly for *you*
not others
even as you
tread the path
of toil
before me
and *for* me

Psalm 25:15   Colossians 3:17   Ephesians 6:7

The Dreaded D's

Lord
in the face of all the
Dreaded D's
of our day

Decadence Deceit Defeat
Defiance Degeneracy Delusion
Depravity Depression Deprivation
Derangement Dereliction Despair
Despondency Destruction Disappointment
Disaster Disbelief Discontent
Discouragement Discrimination Disease
Disenchantment Dishonesty Disillusion
Dismay Disloyalty Disobedience
Disorder Dispute Disquiet
Dissatisfaction Dissension Dissipation
Dissonance Distress Distrust
Disturbance Disunity Doubt
Downheartedness Drudgery Duplicity
DEATH!

From all these
Deliver me
O Lord!
Direct me rather to
Draw near to you
Deny myself
Die to sin
Deepen my commitment
Desire the milk of your Word
Delight in your will
Discover your way
Depend on you
Desire to please you
Be Devoted in prayer
Diligent in service
Daring to risk

Dynamic in Discipleship
Disciplined in Duty
Discerning in Decisions
Discreet in speech
Doing your deeds
Distributing my gifts
Defending the faith
Demonstrating your love
Declaring your gospel
Dedicated in worship
Dwelling in your house
By your grace
Durable unto Death

Romans 12:1,2   Revelation 2:10

Compete with Yourself!

Lord when I am pressured
to compete with others
to win against them
to achieve ahead of them
rather let me
compete with myself
Let me ask
"Am I the person
you want me to be?"
Move me to accept
the limits
of my potential
and then let me
move ahead
in trust
with such gifts
as you have given me
seeking not "success"
but following you
faithfully

Romans 12:3   Revelation 2:10

Coping with Stress —in relation to God

Rock of Ages

I'm always tempted
to make
some kind of a deal
with you
A bargain
on my terms
not yours
Help me to see
that my hands are empty
except for the power
you give me
to cling to the cross
of your Son
Strip me naked
of my own desires
and pretensions
Make me helpless
that I may be
totally dependent
on your
unconditional grace

Ephesians 2:8,9

Pressure from the Prince—of Liars

The Prince of Liars
is pressuring me
to try to
eliminate my guilt
by pretending
it doesn't exist
To *rationalize*
To *justify* myself
Lord move me
to realize
that then
I jeopardize
my bond
with you
A forgiving God
Rather
by your Spirit
convict me of my sin
that I may
truly confess it
and turn it over
to Jesus
the Son of Man
who alone
has power
to forgive
all sin[3]

Psalm 139:23,24   Matthew 9:6

Withdrawal Problems

Lord help me distinguish
between withdrawal *to* you
in prayer
and a withdrawal *from* you
which curves only
inward on my self
Turn me around
Lord
outward
to you
Incline me to
relax
to release
to relinquish myself
totally to you
that your boundless love
may flow again
unchecked
into my heart
and then
that love
flow out
inexhaustibly
through doors of ministry
in service
to others[4]

Colossians 3:16,17

Problems in Prayer

Alert me Lord
to the problems of
misguided prayer
Thinking I have you
in my pocket
or bound in my Bible
Praying with my lips
but not my heart
Hurrying through my devotions
Asking for what I desire
instead of what
you know I need
And suffer me not to pray
"through Jesus Christ"
by rote
thoughtlessly
but let his holy name
purify all that I
think and feel and do
In the strong name of
Jesus Christ

Matthew 26:39

A "Good Christian"?

When I think I am
a "good Christian"
because I am often
compassionate benevolent affable
courteous generous friendly
meek patient temperate
avoiding much evil
worshiping often
frequent in prayer
a reader of devotional books
then cut out the cancer
of my pride
O Lord
Teach me how little
I may know myself
or you
Examine the truth
of my repentance
and my faith
in the gospel
Keep me
from bearing the
name of Christ
in vain
Teach me that
I have not achieved
but *follow after*
Christ

Psalm 139:23,24   Romans 3:23   Philippians 3:12

Praying Improperly

Lord teach me to pray
not from the perspective
of the distorted
and contaminated depths
of my doubts and fears
but as you have
revealed yourself
in your holy Word
Let me first
find you there
and then make my prayer
Let me see you not as
being on vacation
deaf to my cries
needing some encouragement
but that you
knowing what I want
knowing what I need
will give me the grace
and the blessing
through your Holy Spirit
to know what *you* will
for me
in my daily walk
with you
Lord
teach me
not to pray
amiss

Psalm 30:2; 31:21-24   James 4:3

"You Asked For It!"

Lord
teach me
not just
to pray
for what
I want
for
I
may
get
it

Galatians 6:7   Romans 8:26   Matthew 6:10

A Mighty Fortress

Lord
in the midst of battle
against The Enemy
let me not forget
that though you permit
his deadly assaults
you are still in control
The final victory
has already been won
And though I'm still
beset
with problems and
with pain
you're by my side
upon the plain
There is no panic
in Paradise

Psalm 18:1,2; 46

The Means of Grace

Only the
Holy Spirit of God
can teach me
how to pray
I am powerless
until I am plugged in
to your channels of grace
So come to me
O Holy Spirit
in the Scriptures
my Baptism
the Holy Eucharist
Come
Holy Spirit
Come!
And let me
never again be
disconnected

Psalm 143:10   Romans 8:26

My Lips Are Sealed

Move me to talk less
and listen more
Let me be like
faithful Job of old
"I lay my hand
on my mouth"
I bow before you now
in worship and adoration
I await *your* words
not my own
preconceived answers
"Speak Lord
for your servant hears"

Job 40:4   1 Samuel 3:9   Psalm 28:6-9; 38:15; 46:10; 62:1

A Bold Prayer

Lord
I will not let you go
unless you bless me
Let your Word
for my life
not just be
judgment and exposure
of my sin
(I do confess
I do repent
I am a sinful person
O Lord)
but let your Word
be also the Good News
of the reactivating power
of your forgiveness
your goodness
and the
inexhaustible riches of Christ
Let his mercy and power
flow into me
boundlessly
that I may be
transformed
A new creation
I ask this
not timidly
but boldly
in the strong Name
of Jesus Christ[9]

Genesis 32:26   Psalm 51:1-4   2 Corinthians 5:17   James 1:5-7

The Truest Source of Wisdom

In my stress
O Lord
direct me to the truest
source of wisdom
Not only the worship
of the church
sermons soundly preached
rightly dividing
your Word of Truth
Not only the counsel
of Christian friends
or the reading
of prayer books
But direct me
to the holy fountain
of your divinely inspired
Scriptures first of all
Like a newborn baby
let me desire
the sincere milk
of that Word
that I may grow thereby
Let me taste and see
that you are good
receive your Word
with joy
and hold it fast
that Christ may dwell
in me richly
And when all other voices
are silent
may I still hear
your voice
in that Word
and may it abide
in my heart
forever

1 Peter 2:2   Hebrews 6:5   Luke 8:13   Titus 1:9   Colossians 3:16   1 Peter 1:2
Psalm 22:22,25; 26:6-8; 27:4; 84:1-4,10; 122:1; 119:1-72,103,105

Praying the Psalms

In praying through the Psalms
O Lord
I have identified with
the distress of the writer
plagued by enemies
within and without
But let me never forget
O Lord
"the rest of the story"
in the Psalms
that you always
know and *see* my struggle
that you are a God of
steadfast love
that you *answer* prayer
and *deliver* me
in your good time
You *never fail* me
Therefore I *hope* and *trust* in you
I *exult* and *rejoice*
in your *goodness*
Praised be the Name of the Lord!

Psalms 1-150

Bad News

When the enemies
of fear and foreboding
distress doubt and distrust
assail me O Lord
let me not fear
When I expect bad news
or when it comes
let me recall
your abundant mercy
Though you test me
with evil tidings
let me not fall
Keep me on
a calm course
Bear me up
Give me the good news
of your never-failing
steadfast love

Psalm 69:16-18; 66:8-12; 68:19; 69:13; 112:7

Dining Out

The eyes of others
are upon me O Lord
whimsically
as they see me
make my prayer
in this crowded room
> *The eyes of all*
> *wait upon Thee*
Are they thankful
for what they are about
to receive?
> *And Thou givest them their food*
> *in due season*
Their hands are clenched
on a fork or a glass
They feed away
> *Thou openest Thy hand*
> *Thou satisfiest the desire*
> *of every living thing*
Let me never Lord delay
boldly in Thy Name to pray

Psalm 145:15,16   1 Timothy 2:8   Ephesians 5:20

Change and the Unknown

When I fear
the unknown
help me focus
on the Known
you O Lord
When I attempt
to assimilate
the news of the day
the things people say
much of which tends
to intimidate manipulate
militate and dominate me
keep my eyes fixed on
you O Lord
When change dismays me
friends betray me
the world deludes me
and peace eludes me
bind me to the
faithful steadfast
trusted changeless
you O Lord

Psalm 89:33,34; 102:26,27; 136   Malachi 3:6

Not Finding But Being Found

Lord
teach me again
that in one sense
I cannot "find" you
but that
you find me
That only when
I utterly despair
of helping myself
can you begin
to help me
in my time
of great need
So bring me Lord
to the end
of my own strength
that I may
totally rely
on yours[3]

John 15:16   2 Corinthians 12:9

The Real Enemy

In all my affliction
Lord
let me never forget
that you
are not the enemy
Satan is
And though you permit
my pain and stress
you mean it
for good to me
So make me wise
that it be not
my demise
but an instrument
for my growth to
know myself better
love others more
and be drawn
still closer to you
Gird me then Lord
to fight my real foe
and always to know
how pain becomes power
when your strength
by the hour
turns evil
into good
for me

1 Peter 5:8   Genesis 50:20   2 Corinthians 12:10

Putting Stress to Rest

I Forgot About You, God!

It wasn't until
late in the afternoon
that I suddenly realized
I hadn't consciously
thought of you all day Lord
since my morning prayer
What a busy day I had
Too *busy* to remember you?
Forgive me Lord
Of course my faith
was not asleep
I'm still in your care
and grace
even when I'm unconscious
But please help me to be
more aware of your presence
as I study your Word
converse with a Christian friend
enjoy the blessings
of your good earth
and do my work
And thank you Lord
for watching over me
even when I've temporarily
"forgotten" about you

Psalm 34:1; 50:22,23; 71:8,23,24; 103:2; 105:4; 119:93,97

Reflection on the Day

As I look back
upon this day
let me not wallow
in self-pitying remorse
for my sins
but sigh in
true repentance

For pride
for hardness of heart
for complacency
for failure to trust
in your promises
when I faced temptation
or hard decisions
Forgive me
for my self-centeredness
wherever I fell short
of your high calling
And pardon me now
not with the cheap grace
of an easy confession
but through the costly grace
of the shed blood
of your Son
Jesus Christ
my Lord

Psalm 141:1,2; 103:8-12   Romans 6:23

That Secret Closet

Hello again Lord
I knew you
would be waiting for me
in the secret closet
the prayer room
of my innermost heart
Let me come into your presence
with awe
reverence and humility
for I am a sinful person
O Lord
But let me not enter
your company
with fear and timidity
For you are my Friend

and Forgiver
Let me not
just dwell
on my frailties and failures
this day
but on
Your mighty acts
      in temptations overcome
      in friendships increased or restored
Your mighty acts
      in the good you have done in me
      and what good I have done for others
Your mighty acts
      in work completed
      in plans made
Thank you Lord
for another day!

Matthew 6:6   Psalm 71:15,16,19-21; 77:12-15; 126:3; 20:4,5; 21:2 Philippians 2:13

The Pillow of Peace

As this day ends
all that remains
I release to you O Lord
The work I left undone
I release to you O Lord
The friends whose problems
beset me
I release to you O Lord
The loved ones
whose dilemmas
disturb me
I release to you O Lord
The sick whose suffering
grieves me
I release to you O Lord
The fellow workers

whose personalities
perplex me
I release to you O Lord
The clerks who upset
and annoy me
I release to you O Lord
The phone calls which perturb
and bother me
I release to you O Lord
The questions which confuse
and confound me
I release to you O Lord
The fears which alarm
and trouble me
I release to you O Lord
The responsibilities which unsettle
and bewilder me
I release to you O Lord
The obligations which vex
and inconvenience me
I release to you O Lord
All
All
I release to you O Lord
Now let me lay my head back
on the pillow of your peace
and may my last thoughts
be of you

Psalm 4:8; 55:22; 63:5-8   1 Peter 5:7

Riding High!

I'm riding high
right now Lord
But let me be
prepared
for the stress ahead

the valley
after this mountain top
Make me aware
stress can come quickly
at any time
in hidden ways
death
disaster
tragedy in my family
failing health
financial troubles
an unexpected loss
You've met affliction before
Lord Jesus Christ
Let me hear your voice
"Here, Take My Hand"

Psalm 5:8; 23:3; 25:5; 73:23-26; 108:6; 139:7-10   Revelation 7:17

All Through the Night

As I sleep
Lord
spare me from any restlessness
fear and anxiety
which may invade
my dreams
Though Satan never sleeps
remind me that
you don't either
The ultimate victory
has been won
You are in control
So send your angels
to minister to me
as I sleep
Ease my tensions
Renew my body
Restore my soul

that I may awake
refreshed
to live
and work
for you

Psalm 16:7-9; 91:5,11,12; 121:3,4; 127:2; 139:17,18

For this reason, then, I fall on my knees before the Father, from whom every family in heaven and on earth receives its true name. I ask God, from the wealth of his glory, to give you power through his Spirit to be strong in your inner selves, and that Christ will make his home in your hearts, through faith. I pray that you may have your roots and foundations in love, and that you, together with all God's people, may have the power to understand how broad and long and high and deep is Christ's love. Yes, may you come to know his love—although it can never be fully known—and so be completely filled with the perfect fullness of God.

To him who is able to do so much more than we can ever ask for, or even think of, by means of the power working in us: to God be the glory in the church and in Christ Jesus, for all time, for ever and ever! Amen.

Ephesians 3:14-21 (TEV)

References

Baillie, John. *A Diary of Private Prayer.* New York: Charles Scribner's Sons, 1952. A warm and lasting classic which gets between your ribs and explodes inside you. Morning and evening meditations for 31 days. (2)

Brandt, Leslie F. *Meditations on a Loving God.* St. Louis: Concordia Publishing House, 1986. Daily readings through the church year by the well-known author of paraphrases of the psalms and other Scripture in contemporary language.

Deffner, Donald L. *Bound to Be Free: The Quest for Inner Freedom.* Seattle: Morse Press, 1981. Out of print. Copyright Donald L. Deffner. Reprint by Concordia Theological Seminary Press, Ft. Wayne, In. 46825.

Franzmann, Martin H. *Pray for Joy.* St. Louis: Concordia Publishing House, 1970. Thirty richly sculpted imageries celebrating the rhythm and awe of God's good creation. By poet/scholar/hymnodist Martin H. Franzmann, beloved friend who always asked me to play "Bye, Bye, Blackbird" on the piano. (Out of print)

Gill, David W. *The Opening of the Christian Mind.* Downer's Grove, Ill; Inter Varsity Press, 1989. A strong, well-documented call for a spiritually educated laity.

Gockel, Herman W. *What Jesus Means to Me.* St. Louis: Concordia Publishing House, 1956. Hundreds of thousands of copies of this classic have aided Christians in finding their true joy in Christ.

Kolb, Erwin J. *A Prayer Primer.* St. Louis: Concordia Publishing House, 1982. A guide on how to pray in public with pointed aids for personal prayer as well. Clearly and ardently written. Helpful Bible studies included.

Lewis, C. S. *The Joyful Christian.* New York: Macmillan Publishing Company, Inc., 1977. 100 readings from the works of one of the most famous Christian writers of our century.

Lindell, Paul J. *The Mystery of Pain.* Minneapolis: Augsburg Publishing House, 1974. A missionary dying of cancer flings a "handful of stars" to fellow sufferers. Profound Biblical insights on accepting pain, dying every day and praising God for whatever comes. (8) (Out of print)

Mehl, Duane. *At Peace with Failure.* Minneapolis: Augsburg Publishing House, 1984. My affable colleague Duane Mehl reveals his personal struggle in candidly describing how God gives grace to live beyond shattered dreams. (3)

Peterson, Eugene H. *Working the Angles: The Shape of Pastoral Integrity.* Grand Rapids, Mich.: William B. Eerdmans Publishing Company, 1988. A call to the clergy and laity to recognize the pastoral vocation as being that of prayer, Scripture, and spiritual direction.

Phillips, J. B. *The Newborn Christian.* New York: Macmillan Publishing Company, Inc., 1978. 114 readings from the rich literary lore of the famous canon. (9)

The Stress Kit: A Positive Approach to Stress Management. Appleton, WI: The Aid Association for Lutherans, 1987. (10)

Wold, Margaret. *The Critical Moment.* Minneapolis: Augsburg Publishing House, 1978. An exceptional volume by an exceptional woman who sees crisis and struggle as the contact point for enrichment rather than despair. Marge shares the agony of her husband's paralyzing accident, and the traumatic stress experiences of many other women as well. (4) (Out of print)